The Vegetarian Journey

Rice Trail

Anita Gupta

notionpress
.com

INDIA · SINGAPORE · MALAYSIA

Notion Press

Old No. 38, New No. 6
McNichols Road, Chetpet
Chennai - 600 031

First Published by Notion Press 2020
Copyright © Anita Gupta 2020
All Rights Reserved.

ISBN 978-1-64783-579-8

Dedicated to

My Family and
Friends

Contents

Salads

1. Rice Noodles Salad

2. Sunshine Salad

3. Three Rice Salad

4. Fattoush (Mid East Salad)

5. Raw Poha Salad

6. Cauliflower & Broccoli Salad

7. Purple Cabbage and Bok Choy & Corn

8. Thai Style Broccoli and Apple Salad

9. Broccoli Chickpea Carrot Salad

10. Broccoli & Rice Noodle Salad

11. Assorted Green Walnut Crouton Salad

12. Marinated Vegetable Salad

13. Corn Whole Beans Salad

14. Rice and Vegetable Salad

15. Friends Favourite Salad

Rice Noodles Salad

SERVING SIZE : 7-8

INGREDIENTS

- 100 gm thin Rice Noodles (Soaked in boiling water and salt for 10 minutes and drained)
- 200 gm Chickpea (boiled)
- 2 Cucumbers (chopped in small Pcs)
- 2 Tomatoes (remove seeds and chop)
- 200 gm Water Chestnut (boiled and finely sliced)
- 1/2 cup fresh Basil Leaves
- 100 gm Spinach (roughly chopped)
- 3 to 4 Spring Onions (finely chopped)
- 1/2 cup roasted Peanuts (coarsely ground)

INGREDIENTS FOR DRESSING

- 1 cup water
- 1 tbsp. sweet Chili sauce
- 2 tbsp. Apple Cider Vinegar
- 1 tbsp. Lemon juice
- 1 ½ tsp. Corn flour
- Salt and Pepper to taste

FOR PREPARATION

Boil ¾ cup of water, in the remaining ¼ cup water mix the corn flour along with the other ingredients. Add to the boiling water till it thickens, switch off the gas stove and cool the dressing.

Mix the rice noodles along with the Chickpeas and other vegetables etc. Add the dressing just before serving. Garnish with basil leaves and ground peanuts and serve.

NUTRITIONAL VALUE (Approx)

Calories 310, carbohydrate 56 gm, protein 28.6 gm

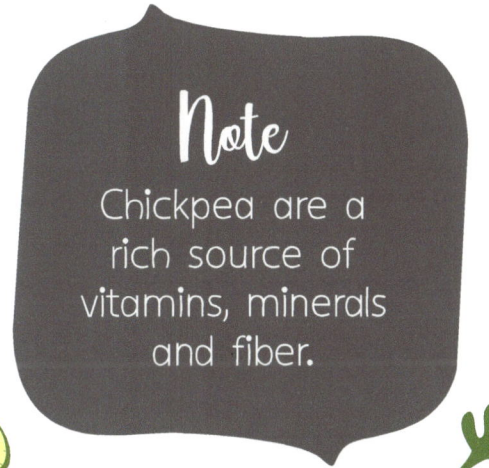

Note

Chickpea are a rich source of vitamins, minerals and fiber.

Sunshine Salad

SERVING SIZE : 6-8

INGREDIENTS

- 2 heads Broccoli (cut into small pcs and lightly steamed)
- 1 large Capsicum (roasted and cut in cubes without seeds)
- 2 large Yellow Capsicum (roasted and cut in strips)
- 2 Carrots (cut in shape of matchsticks)
- 2 Potatoes (cut into finger chips and roasted in an oven or air fryer)
- 2 Tomatoes (deseeded and cut in cubes)
- 15 to 20 tender Spinach Leaves roughly chopped
- 2 to 3 Beet root (steamed for 8 to 10 minutes in a microwave. And then cut in thin long pcs)
- Dry Fruits eg. walnuts, pecans, almonds(roasted and crushed coarsely)

INGREDIENTS FOR DRESSING

- 2 tbsp. Olive oil
- 1 tbsp. fresh Rosemary (finely Chopped)
- 1 tsp. Salt
- 1/4 tsp. black Pepper
- 2 tbsp. Lemon juice
- 1-2 Onions (finely sliced and marinated with salt + lemon juice for 1/2 hour)

FOR PREPARATION

Add the ingredients for dressing in a mixing bowl. Add all the prepared vegetables along with the roasted finger chips. Mix well and serve after garnishing it with roasted dry fruits.

NUTRITIONAL VALUE (Approx)

Calories: 232 per serve.

Note

Broccoli is high in Vitamin C, K, iron and potassium. Raw Broccoli is 90% water.

Three Rice Salad

SERVING SIZE : 7-8

INGREDIENTS

- 1 cup cooked Brown Rice
- 1/2 cup cooked Black Rice
- 1 cup cooked White Rice
- 3/4 cup Spring Onion (finely chopped)
- 1 cup fresh Spinach roughly torn
- 1 cup boiled Peas
- 2 Tomatoes (deseeded and cut into small cubes)
- 1 head Lettuce (save few leaves for garnishing)
- 1 Onion (finely chopped)
- 1/4 cup Almonds (roasted and chopped)
- 1/2 cup Yogurt (for dressing)
- 2 to 3 tbsp. Olive oil
- 1 tbsp. Ginger paste
- 1 to 2 tsp. Mustard sauce
- 2 tbsp. Vinegar
- Salt and Pepper to taste
- 2 tbsp. Lemon juice
- 1-2 tbsp. Jaggery Syrup or Honey

FOR PREPARATION

Mix together all the 3 rice, green, onion, spinach, boiled pea and tomatoes. In a bowl take the dressing ingredients and mix them very well. Before garnishing the dish, Mix dressing and rice combination Serve the salad on a bed of lettuce leaves.

NUTRITIONAL VALUE (Approx)

Calories160, Carbohydrates 34gm, protein 25.4gm, fat 11.7 gm

Fattoush
(Mid East Salad)

SERVING SIZE : 3-4

INGREDIENTS

- 15 to 20 fresh Lettuce Leaves (washed, cleaned and roughly torn)
- 1 Cucumber (sliced in rounds)
- 2 Tomatoes (cubed without seeds)
- 1 Red Capsicum (Cut in cubes)
- 1 Green Capsicum (Cut in small cubes)
- 2 Thin Flat Bread or Pita (toasted lightly)
- 1 to 2 tbsp. Lemon juice
- 1 to 2 tbsp. Olive Oil
- 1 to 2 tsp. Garlic Clove (minced)
- 2 tsp. Cumin (roasted)
- 1 tbsp. Pomegranate Molasses/Sugar
- 1 tsp. Salt
- Pepper to taste
- 1 tbsp. Zatar

Zatar:- Zatar is a Mediterranean spice for salad etc. Its Ingredients are:-

- 7-8 tbsp. Thyme dried
- 2 tsp. Marjoram dried
- 3-4 tsp. Sesame seeds roasted
- 2 tsp. sumac (Indian amchur can be used)
- 1 tsp. salt
- Powder all together and sprinkle on salad as needed, store the rest in a glass jar

FOR PREPARATION

Tear the lettuce leaves into small pieces. Spread on a dish along with sliced cucumber, tomatoes, capsicum and sprinkle olive oil, salt, pepper, pomegranate and zatar. Toast pita bread lightly and cut into bite size pcs, spread on salad and serve.

NUTRITIONAL VALUE (Approx)

Calories 164, Carbohydrates 15.2 gm, Protein 2.7 gm

Raw Poha Salad

SERVING SIZE : 2-3

INGREDIENTS

- 1 cup Poha or beaten rice
- 1/2 cup boiled Peas
- 1 cup Carrot (grated)
- 1 cup Cabbage (grated or finely chopped)
- 1 tsp. oil
- 1 tsp. Cumin (roasted)
- 2 tbsp. Lemon juice
- 10 to 15 Curry leaves
- 1/4 cup Peanuts (roasted or fried)
- Salt and pepper to taste
- 2 tsp. Sugar
- 1/4 tsp. Chili powder
- 2 tbsp. Coriander leaves
- 2-3 tbsp. fresh Coconut (grated)

FOR PREPARATION

Wash the Poha in a sieve and keep it aside. Take ¾ cup water, ½ tsp. salt, 2 tbsp. lemon juice and 1 tsp. sugar. Now, soak the poha in this water till it is absorbed. Keep aside. In a pan heat oil and then add the mustard and curry leaves, stir well and then add the carrot and cabbage. Fry for 1-2 mins. Switch off the gas stove and mix the poha along with the vegetables, pea and lemon juice. Mix well and serve cool garnished with peanuts, grated coconut and coriander leaves.

NUTRITIONAL VALUE
(Approx)

Calories 165, Protein 7 gm, Fat 7.03 gm

Note

Poha is a good source of carbohydrates, iron, fiber and antioxidants.

Cauliflower & Broccoli Salad

SERVING SIZE : 4-5

INGREDIENTS

- 400 gm Cauliflower (cut in small pcs.)
- 200 gm Broccoli (cut in small bite size pcs.)
- 1 tsp. Black and 1 tsp. White Sesame Seeds (lightly roasted)

INGREDIENTS FOR DRESSING

- 1/2 cup Tomato Ketchup
- 1/2 tsp. Hot Chili Sauce
- 1 tbsp. Brown Sugar
- 1 tbsp. Mustard Sauce
- 1 tbsp. Soy Sauce
- 1 tbsp. Apple Cider
- 1/2 tsp. Salt
- 1/2 tsp. Pepper

FOR PREPARATION

Boil enough water to blanch the cauliflower and broccoli. Add salt to the boiling water. Soak the florets in this hot water and strain after 2-3 minutes. Then wash with cold water and keep aside. Mix all the dressing ingredients except sesame seeds. Mix the florets and dressing very well and serve garnished with both sesame seeds.

NUTRITIONAL VALUE (Approx)

Calories 207, Protein 28.6 gm

Purple Cabbage and Bok Choy & Corn

SERVING SIZE : 4-5

INGREDIENTS

- 200 gm Purple Cabbage (shredded)
- 100 gm Corn kernels (boiled)
- 200 gm Bok Choy (roughly torn)
- 100 gm Carrots (cut in form of matchstick)

INGREDIENTS FOR DRESSING

- 1 tbsp. Maple syrup / honey/Jaggery syrup
- 2 tbsp. Apple cider vinegar
- 2 tbsp. Lemon juice
- 1/8 tbsp. red chilli powder
- Salt and Pepper to taste

FOR PREPARATION

Combine very well all the vegetables. Mix the dressing ingredients, in a bowl. Toss the dressing in vegetables and serve.

Note

Purple Cabbage is rich in Vitamin -K, Vitamin-C, Vitamin B-6, and Bokchoy is low in calories good source of dietary fiber.

Thai Style Broccoli and Apple Salad

SERVING SIZE : 6-7

INGREDIENTS

- 500 gm Broccoli (Cut in small florets and steamed)
- 2 Apple (finely chopped)
- 2 to3 Tomatoes cut in cubes (optional)
- 2 to 3 tbsp. Sunflower seeds.
- 2 tbsp. Raisin
- 1-2 tsp Garlic minced
- tbsp. Olive oil
- 2-3 tbsp. Lemon juice
- 2-3 tbsp. Garlic Cloves minced
- 1/2 tsp. Cumin Powder
- 1 to 2 tbsp. Sesame seeds (dry roasted)
- 2 tbsp. Water
- 1/2 cup toasted Bread (crumbled later)
- Salt and Black Pepper to taste

FOR PREPARATION

Mix together Olive oil, Lemon Juice, Garlic, Cumin, water, Apple, Broccoli and Tomatoes add bread crumbs transfer to a serving bowl garnish with Raisin, Sunflower seeds and Sesame seeds. Serve immediately.

When seeds like sunflower, sesame are toasted they give good, crunch, taste and aroma.

NUTRITIONAL VALUE (Approx)

Calories 204, Carbohydrates 33gm, Protein 2.8 gm

Note
Broccoli lowers the risk of cancer it is nutrient dense and contains large amount of Vitamin-C.

Broccoli Chickpea Carrot Salad

SERVING SIZE : 3-4

INGREDIENTS

- 2 to 3 cups Broccoli florets steamed
- 1 ½ cup boiled Chickpea
- 2 Carrots shredded or (cut in bite size pieces)
- 2 to 3 Tomatoes (cut in small cubes)
- 2 to 3 tbsp. Balsamic Vinegar
- 2 tbsp. Apple Cider
- 2 tbsp. Maple Syrup/ Honey/ Jaggery syrup
- 1 to 2 tbsp. Lemon Juice
- Salt and Pepper to taste
- 2 tbsp. Coriander (finely chopped)

FOR PREPARATION

In a bowl mix together, all the dressing ingredients except coriander. Add the chickpea, broccoli, carrot, tomato. Now mix very well garnish with coriander leaves, transfer to a serving bowl garnish with Coriander. Serve immediately.

NUTRITIONAL VALUE (Approx)

Calories 256, Carbohydrate 33 gm, Protein 2.8 gm, fat 2.6 gm

Broccoli & Rice Noodle Salad

SERVING SIZE : 6-8

INGREDIENTS

- 2 cup Broccoli (cut in bite size florets and steam)
- 150 gm Rice Noodles (soaked in boiling water for 10-12mins. and strained)
- 2 Cucumbers (finely chopped)
- 2 Tomatoes (finely chopped)
- 3-4 Orange(Segments separated)
- 1/2 cup Peanuts (roasted and coarsely crushed)
- 10-15 Basil leaves (roughly torn)

INGREDIENTS FOR DRESSING

- 2-3 tbsp. Olive oil
- 1/4 tsp. chilli powder
- 2 tbsp. Honey
- 2-3 tbsp. Apple Cider
- Salt and Pepper to taste
- 2 tbsp. Roasted Peanuts (finely crushed)

FOR PREPARATION

In a large bowl mix together broccoli, cucumber, rice noodles, tomatoes, orange segments and peanuts together. Take another bowl for dressing, mix together. Olive oil, Honey Apple Cider, Salt and Pepper add this preparation to the vegetables. Stir well transfer it to a serving bowl. Garnish with peanuts and basil leaves before serving.

NUTRITIONAL VALUE
(Approx)

Calories 245,carbohydrate 36 gm, Protein 7 gm, Fat 11 gm

Assorted Green Walnut Crouton Salad

SERVING SIZE : 4-5

INGREDIENTS

- 200 gm baby Spinach
- 100 gm Aragula or Raddish tender leaves
- 100 gm Lettuce
- 1/2cup roasted Walnuts
- A hand full bread Crouton

INGREDIENTS FOR DRESSING

- 1-2 tbsp. Balsamic Vinegar
- Salt and Pepper to taste
- 1-2 tbsp. Lemon Juice (Optional)
- 1tbsp. Olive oil
- 2 tbsp. Garlic minced(optional)
- 1-2 whole red chili broken

FOR PREPARATION

Heat oil in a pan and fry garlic along with red chili. Add the aragula or raddish leaves and lightly stir fry on high flame for a few minutes (2-3 minutes) add salt, pepper switch off the gas stove. Transfer to dish add balsamic vinegar, walnut and crouton just before serving.

NUTRITIONAL VALUE (Approx)

Calories 220, Carbohydrate 22 gm, Protein 13 gm.

Marinated Vegetable Salad

SERVING SIZE : 5-6

INGREDIENTS

- 1 cup French Beans (cut in 1" pcs and steamed for 4-5 mins. Then given a cold bath)
- 1 ½ cup Cabbage (shredded)
- 4-5 Carrots roughly (grated, extract extra moisture)
- 1 pc Cucumber (chopped)
- 2-3 garlic cloves (minced)
- 1 cup Green Moong (lightly steamed)

INGREDIENTS FOR DRESSING

- 1 Onion (sliced)
- 3 tbsp. Brown Sugar
- 2-3 tbsp. Apple Cider
- 1 tsp. Salt
- 1/8 tsp. Black Pepper
- 1-2 tbsp. Lemon juice

FOR PREPARATION

Mix all the dressing ingredients in a bowl. Then add the beans, onion, garlic, cabbage, moong. Add carrots and cucumber in the end. Mix the preparation very well and serve immediately.

When beans are steamed their colour changes but the cold bath returns its colour add ½ tsp sugar white steaming.

NUTRITIONAL VALUE (Approx)

Calories : 150.

Corn Whole Beans Salad

SERVING SIZE : 4-5

INGREDIENTS

- 1 cup Sweet Corn (boiled)
- 1 cup whole Beans (, Moong /Lobia)
- 2 pcs Tomatoes (deseeded and cubed)
- 2 pcs Onions (finely chopped)
- 2 tbsp. Coriander (finely chopped)
- 1 Red Capsicum (cut in small cubes)
- 1 cup Spinach (roughly torn)

INGREDIENTS FOR DRESSING

- 1/2 tsp. Black pepper
- 1 tsp. Salt
- 2 tbsp. Olive oil
- 2-3 tbsp. Lemon juice
- 1-2 tsp. Jaggery syrup or Honey

FOR PREPARATION

Mix all the dressing ingredients in a bowl. Combine the beans, corn and all vegetables together. Mix the dressing and vegetables very well. Transfer to serving plate and garnish with coriander and serve.

NUTRITIONAL VALUE (Approx)

Calories- 150, Protein-2gm

Note

This is a very easy and eye catching salad. Corn is high in carbohydrates but packed with fiber, vitamins, minerals and antioxidants. Vegetables can be changed as per choice.

Rice and Vegetable Salad

SERVING SIZE : 6-7

INGREDIENTS

- 1 cup Brown Rice (boiled)
- 1 cup White Rice (boiled)
- 1 cup Radish (grated)
- 1/2 cup green Onion (chopped)
- 1 Carrot (shredded)
- 1 Green Capsicum (finely cut)
- 1/2 Yellow Bell Pepper (roasted and finely cut)
- 1Red Pepper(roasted and finely cut)

INGREDIENTS FOR DRESSING

- 1/4 cup Basil/Celery Fresh
- 1/4 Cup Thick Yogurt
- 2 tbsp. Soy Sauce
- 1 tbsp. Lemon juice
- Salt and Pepper to taste
- 1/8 tsp. Red Chili Powder

FOR PREPARATION

In a bowl mix together ingredients for dressing except basil or celery. Now add all the above vegetables in a large mixing bowl, except red pepper and stir well. Mix the dressing evenly in the vegetable bowl.

Garnish, with basil and red pepper and serve it.

NUTRITIONAL VALUE (Approx)

Calories : 250.

Note

Radish in high in nutrients, packed with vitamins E, A, B6 and K. Zinc, Fiber, Potassium, Phosphorous, Magnesium and Copper, it improves digestion.

This is a complete meal with the goodness of rice and lots of vegetables.

Friends Favourite Salad

SERVING SIZE : 6-8

INGREDIENTS

- 200 gm Split Moong Dal (soaked for 2 to 3 hours, then boiled with each grain separate)
- 200 gm Paneer or Cottage cheese or firm Tofu (cut in small cubes)
- 1 hand full Cranberries
- 1 bunch Spinach (finely chopped)
- 2 tbsp. Coriander (finely chopped)
- 2 tbsp. Broken Cashew (roasted)

INGREDIENTS FOR DRESSING

- 3-4 tbsp. Lemon Juice
- 1 tsp. Cumin (roasted)
- 1/2 tsp. Black Pepper
- 1/2 tsp. Red Chilli Powder
- 1 ¼ tsp. Salt
- Mix together all the ingredients for dressing

NUTRITIONAL VALUE (Approx)

Calories 235.

FOR PREPARATION

Soak the moong dal for 2 hours. In a heavy pan add just enough water to boil the moong. Keep checking in between so that the dal is not over cooked. Each grain remains separate. In another pan boil the pea till tender. Cut the paneer in small pcs and shred the spinach. Dry roast the cashews and cut them in quarters. Trim the coriander and finely chop it. In a large bowl, add all the above ingredients along with the dressing and mix it well with the help of a fork. Serve immediately, after garnishing it with coriander.

Note

Moong dal is extremely nutritious it gets digested easily without producing toxins. Paneer or cottage cheese is an important part of the Indian cuisine. It is nourishing and healthy especially for vegetarians.

Soups

Corn and Red, Capsicum Soup

SERVING SIZE : 6-7

INGREDIENTS

- 400 gm Corn Kernels
- 2 Red Capsicums (Cut in Small Pieces without seeds)
- 2-3 Onions (finely chopped)
- 2 Red Chillies (chopped)
- 1/2 Red, Green, Yellow Capsicums each (finely chopped)
- 1 tsp. Fresh Rosemary
- 600 ml vegetable stock, or water
- Salt and Pepper to taste
- 30 gm Butter
- 2 tbsp. Olive oil
- 1 tbsp. Coriander leaves (finely chopped)
- 2-3 tbsp. lemon juice

FOR PREPARATION

Heat olive oil and melt half of the butter in a pan on low flame add the onions and saute. Now add the red capsicum and stir fry for 3-4 mins. Add the stock and stir well. Cook for 20-25 minutes keeping covered and stirring in between.

Meanwhile, take another pan and heat the remaining butter and fry the capsicum (yellow and green). Let it cook for 3-4 mins. Then switch off the gas stove.

When the onion, capsicum are ready, puree them in a mixer jar. Transfer the content of the jar to a pan. Add salt, pepper and if the consistency is thick add some water or stock. Now add the sauted capsicum in the soup and serve hot garnished with coriander leaves.

NUTRITIONAL VALUE (Approx)

Calories: 225

Note

Capsicum are rich in vitamin-C and A it also has analgesic and anti inflammatory properties.

Carrot and Onion Soup

SERVING SIZE : 6-8

INGREDIENTS

- 500 gm Carrots (washed peeled and cut in cubes)
- 1 to 2 onions sliced
- 2 bay leaves
- 2 to 3 cloves Garlic (Optional)
- 3 to 4 tbsp White Rice(boiled)
- 1 tsp. Cummin(roasted ground)
- 1 tsp. dry Coriander(ground)
- Salt and Pepper to taste
- 1 tsp. Paprika Powder
- 6 to 7 cups Water
- 2 tbsp. fresh Coriander (chopped)
- 2 to 3 Tbsp. Lemon Juice and 1 Tsp. Lemon zest
- 2 Tbsp. Basil fresh leaves
- 2 Tbsp. Butter or Olive Oil

FOR PREPARATION

Add butter or olive oil in a pan on low flame. Add Onions, Garlic and fry for 2 minutes. Add bay leaves then carrots and water/ stock cover and cook till the carrots are soft. When cool remove the bay leaves and churn the carrot mix in a mixer. Transfer to the pot, add paprika powder, coriander, black pepper and salt. Boil for 8 to 10 minutes. In a small bowl, mix the basil, lemon juice and lemon zest and add a pinch of salt. Serve the soup with 1-2 tsp. boiled white rice and a tsp. Lemon Basil dressing.

NUTRITIONAL VALUE (Approx)

Calories: 145.

Pho
(A Vietnamese Meal in a Bowl Soup)

SERVING SIZE : 5-6

INGREDIENTS

- 1 cup Moong Beans (sprout)
- 100 gm of Mushrooms (Separate the stem and cut in quarters)
- Mushroom stems (roughly chopped)
- 2 Onions(quartered)
- 3" Ginger (grated)
- 2 to 3 Turnips or bottle ground (peeled and cut in wedges)
- 3 to 4 Carrots (sliced finely)
- 6 to 8 Garlic cloves (minced)
- 4 to 5 Lemon Grass stalks
- 100 gm of Cauliflower (cut in florets)
- 2 to 3 Green Peppers (slit)
- 100 gm Tofu (cut in cubes)
- 100 gm Rice Noodles (soaked in boiling water strained)
- 6 to 8 Spring Onions (finely chopped)
- 1 cup fresh Coriander (chopped)
- 1/2 cup Basil (roughly torn)
- 2 tbsp. Mint Leaves
- 1 tbsp. Oil
- 4 to 5 Star Anise, 5 to 6 Clove whole 15 to 20 pieces of Pepper Corns and 1"Cinnamom
- 2 to 3 tbsp. Lemon juice
- 6 pieces Lemon wedges
- 100 gm of White Rice
- 2 tbsp. brown Sugar
- Salt to taste

FOR PREPARATION

Take oil in a large pan and add star anise, cloves, pepper, corn, cinnamon and lemon grass stalks. Add onions, turnip, mushrooms, carrot, half of grated ginger and minced garlic. Stir for 3 to 4 minutes and then add water and let it boil. Now add the cauliflower, beans sprouts and the green pepper. Boil for another 4 to 5 minutes. Add salt and rice noodles, 3 cups of water and boil for a few minutes. Add the tofu, coriander, basil and mint, brown sugar, and the Rice. Serve with Lemon juice and Lemon wedges.

Almond Chickpea Soup

SERVING SIZE : 4-6

INGREDIENTS

- 200 gm Chickpea (soaked overnight)
- 75 gm almonds or cashew(soaked)
- 2 tbsp. Olive Oil or Butter
- 2 Onions (finely chopped)
- 2-3 Garlic Cloves (minced)
- 1" grated Ginger
- Salt and Pepper to taste
- Mint for garnish
- 1 - 2 tsp. Lemon juice
- 1 cup boiled white rice
- 1 cup Milk

FOR PREPARATION

Pressure cook the Chickpea in 500 ml water with a little salt, for 12-15mins till they are soft. In a heavy bottom, pan add butter or olive oil and fry the onions, minced garlic and grated ginger. Churn the Chickpea and almonds separately in a mixer jar (save a few for garnish). Now add the onions. Add water and milk. Boil add salt and pepper. l. Serve hot, garnished with almonds and 1 tbsp. of boiled rice mint and lemon juice.

NUTRITIONAL VALUE (Approx)

Calories : 200 Per Serving

Creamy Peanut Soup

SERVING SIZE : 4-6

INGREDIENTS

- 1 cup shelled Peanuts (soaked overnight)
- 1-2 tbsp. Olive oil or ground nut oil
- 1/4 tsp. Nutmeg powder
- 2 onions (finely sliced)
- 2-3 clove garlic (minced)
- 1 tsp. ginger (grated)
- 1 tbsp. Peanut powder or Peanut Butter (optional)
- 1 tsp. Lemon Zest
- 1 cup Coconut Milk
- 2 boiled Potato (cubed)
- 2 Tomatoes (finely cubed without seeds)
- 1/8 tsp. Cayenne Pepper
- 2-3 tbsp. Lemon juice
- Mint and roasted Peanuts (for garnishing)

FOR PREPARATION

Add oil in a pan and fry the onions, minced garlic and grated ginger. Add the soaked peanuts and stir for a while (5-7 minutes). Now, add water and cover to cook for 10 minutes. Cool and grind in the mixer jar. Transfer to a pan and boil with coconut milk, add salt, pepper, nutmeg and lemon Zest. Serve hot with potato and tomato cubes and fresh lemon juice, mint and roasted peanuts.

NUTRITIONAL VALUE (Approx)

Calories -220 per serving

Winter Lentil Soup

SERVING SIZE : 6-7

INGREDIENTS

- 1 ½ cup Red Pigeon Pea (Lal masoor washed and soaked)
- 1 Carrot(chopped)
- 1 Potato (chopped)
- 2 Onions (finely chopped and crispy fried in oil)
- 2-3 Clove Garlic (minced)
- 1 tsp. Ginger (grated)
- 2 Bay leaves
- 2 Star Anise
- Salt and Pepper to taste
- 2-3 tbsp. Lemon juice
- Mint and Coriander (to garnish)
- 1-2 tsp. Roasted Cumin
- 1-2 tbsp. fried Peanuts (coarsely crushed)

FOR PREPARATION

Take Pigeon pea (dal) Carrot, Potato, minced garlic, grated ginger, Bay Leaf, Star Anise. Add 4 cups water and boil giving at least (2-3 whistle) let it cool. Strain it in a sieve, boil again with salt, pepper, Cummin, lemon juice, coriander, fry onion and pepper for 5-7 minutes, if the soup is thick add some boiled water. Serve with lemon juice and crushed peanuts.

NUTRITIONAL VALUE (Approx)

Calories 235

Note

Red pigeon (Lal Masoor) is low in Cholesterol, contains high level of Protein, Amino acids and Potassium and iron. Easy on digestion.

Kumaon Dubka Soup

SERVING SIZE : 3-4

INGREDIENTS

- 1 cup yellow Moong soaked for 2-3 hours (then grind in a mixer jar with some water)
- 2-3 Onions
- 4-5 Garlic
- 1" Ginger
- 1 whole Red chilli dry
- 1 tbsp. whole Coriander
- 1 tsp. Black Pepper whole
- 2 tsp. (Jeera)Cumin
- 4-5 Tomato(ground)
- 2 tbsp. Mustard oil

Grind together

FOR PREPARATION

Heat oil in a heavy pan add onions stir fry for 3-4 min. Now add the ground spice mix and continue to stir at this stage keep the stove flame low. When the spices are aromatic add pureed tomato cook for 3-5 min. Now the ground dal and water go in the pan, boil for 10-12 min checking in between for water level add more if needed. Garnish with roasted cumin powder fresh coriander and lemon wedges.

Onion Shorba

SERVING SIZE : 3-4

INGREDIENTS

- 4-5 Onions large cut in pieces
- 6-8 Spring Onion chopped (both green and white part)
- 3 cups Milk
- 3-4 Garlic cloves
- 1/4 tsp. Black pepper
- Salt to taste
- 2 tbsp Butter
- 1 ½ tsp Fresh or dried Rosemary
- 3 cups Water

FOR PREPARATION

In a heavy bottom pan add 1 tbsp of butter and fry the onions on low flame along with the spring onions and garlic for 4-5 minutes. Add water and boil for 5 minutes then switch off the gas stove and cool. Grind in a mixer jar. Transfer to a pan, add milk and salt, pepper and the herbs boil for 5-7 minutes. Serve hot with lemon slice and a dash of butter.

NUTRITIONAL VALUE (Approx)

Iron 22%; Fat 25 gm; Fiber 7.5 gm; Calories 230

Biryanis

1. Cauliflower Biryani

2. Mushroom Biryani

3. Nutri Nugget and Methi Pakora (Dumpling) Biryani

4. Roasted Eggplant Biryani

5. Paneer Biryani

Cauliflower Biryani

SERVING SIZE : 5-7

INGREDIENTS FOR RICE

- 350 gm long Grain Rice (Wash several times and soak for 1 hrs)
- 4-6 pcs. green Cardamom
- 4-6 pcs Clove
- 7-8 pcs whole Black Pepper
- 2" pcs Cinnamon
- 2 Pcs Bay Leaf
- 2-3 Pcs Star Anise
- 1 tbsp. Ghee (Clarified Butter)
- 2 tsp. Salt
- 2 tsp. Cummin

INGREDIENTS FOR PUREE

- 500 gm Tomatoes
- 1 tbsp. Ghee/Oil
- 1 tsp. Cumin whole raw
- 1 tsp. Garam Masala
- 1 tsp. Chili Powder
- 1 tsp. Sugar

INGREDIENTS FOR CAULIFOLWER

- 800 gm Cauliflower (cut in even size florets)
- 1 cup hung Curd
- 1 tbsp. Ginger grated
- 4-5 pcs Garlic clove minced
- 2 pcs Onion (finely chopped)
- 1 pc Green Chili
- 2 tsp. Garam Masala
- 2 tsp. Red Chili powder
- 2 tsp. Salt
- 2-3 tsp. Biryani Masala
- 1 tsp. Chat Masala
- 1 tsp. Saunf (fennel)ground
- 2 tbsp. Ghee / oil
- 1 tbsp. Corn flour / Gram flour (Besan)
- 2 -3 tbsp lemon juice

PERPRATION FOR RICE

In a pan heat ghee add the Cumin and all the whole Spices stir for a minute add water and boil. Now add the rice and salt. When the rice is 85%boiled strain it. With a fork open the rice so that each grain is separate.

FOR MARINATING CAULIFLOWER

Boil sufficient water in a pan with 1 tsp salt add the cauliflower when the water boils. Strain after 3-4 mins. In a large bowl combine together hung curd, lemon juice, chilli powder, salt, biryani masala, chat masala, saunf (fennel) powder, ginger, garlic and onions. Now mix the corn flour or gram (besan). Add blanched cauliflower sir well to coat it well. Leave it covered for 30 min to marinate.

In a pan heat the oil/Ghee add cumin when it splutters add the marinated cauliflower cover and cook for 5-7 mins stir in between lightly.

FOR THE PUREE

Soak the tomatoes in boiling water for a few minutes. Now strain the blanched tomatoes. Remove the skin when a little cool. Grind in a mixer jar. In a pan heat oil add cumin, tomato puree, salt, garam masala,chilli powder and sugar. Boil till it is a thick puree. Add 1 tsp biryani masala.

TO ASSEMBLE BIRYANI

In a handi / borosil bowl or earthen pot spread half the rice and layer it with the marinated cauliflower.Spread some tomato puree on it, layer with rice and cauliflower.Now cover with the remaining rice.Sprinkle saffron milk and garam masala, fried onions. Bake in a pre heated oven for 12-15 min.Serve garnished with mint,accompanied by papad,chutney and pickle of choice.

TOTAL NUTRITIONAL VALUE

Calories 310, Carbohydrate 80,
Protein 25.5 gm.

Cauliflower is packed with fiber and bone boosting vitamin K

Mushroom Biryani

SERVING SIZE : 5-7

INGREDIENTS FOR MUSHROOM

- 500 gm large Mushroom (cleaned and cut in halves)
- 4-5 Tomatoes pureed
- 1 cup Thick Yogurt
- 3 Onions (finely chopped)
- 2 Spring Onion (finely chopped)
- 200 gm Ginger shredded
- 5-6 Garlic Cloves minced
- 1 Capsicum (finely chopped)
- 1 tsp. Chili Powder
- ½ tsp. Turmeric Powder
- 1 ½ tsp. Garam Masala
- 2 tsp. Biryani Masala
- 2 tsp. Cumin (ground)
- 2-3 tsp. Thick Cream (optional)

FOR THE RICE

- 3 cup Rice(washed and soaked for 1 hour
- 2 tsp. Salt
- 1 tbsp. Vegetable oil/Ghee
- 2 Bay Leaf
- 2-3 Black Cardamom
- 4-6 Green Cardamom
- 5-6 Cloves
- 8-10 Black Pepper

FOR GARNISHING

- 1 tbsp Cumin
- A few strands Saffron soaked in 2 tbsp milk
- A pinch of cardamom powder

FOR PREPARATION

Heat Oil or ghee add the cumin and all the whole spices with enough water to boil the rice. When the water boils add the rice and cook until it is nearly done strain then keep aside.

FOR PREPARATION FOR MUSHROOM

Heat oil and add the onion, in a minute add spring onion ginger capsicum stir for 2-3 min. Add the tomato puree and keep stirring for few minutes. Now add the yogurt, mix well add the spices if using cream add to the mix. Add the mushrooms and cook for 4-5 minutes switch off the gas.

TO ASSEMBLE

Spread a layer of rice then the mushroom mix then the rice- sprinkle milk with saffron. Garnish with coriander and fried onion bake for 20-25 min, serve hot with salan or tomato chutney and papad..

NUTRITIONAL VALUE (Approx)

Protein 10.8 g; Fat 4.2 g; Carbohydrate 71.0 g; Cholesterol 5.5 mg; Calories 344.1 cal.

Nutri Nugget and Methi Pakora (Dumpling) Biryani

SERVING SIZE : 8-10

INGREDIENTS FOR METHI PAKORA

- 200 gm fresh tender Methi Leaves (fenugreek leaves) (finely chopped)
- 70 gm gram flour (Besan)
- 1 tsp. Salt
- 1/2 tsp. Red Chili Powder
- 1 tsp. Ginger & Green Chili Paste
- Oil for frying
- 200 gm Nutri Nugget or Soya Nugget (Soaked in water for 1-2 hrs. then strained well)
- 400 gm Basmati Rice or Basmati Long Grain Rice (washed well and soaked in water for 1 hr)
- 1 tbsp. Ghee
- 4-6 Cloves
- 6-8 Black Pepper
- 2-3 Brown Cardamom
- 4-5 Green Cardamom
- 2 Bay Leaf
- 1" Cinnamon
- 1 tsp. Salt
- 2 tsp. Cumin

INGREDIENTS FOR MASALA

- 500 gm Tomato (cut in small cubes and puree in mixer)
- 2 tbsp. Ginger Garlic & Green Chili Paste
- 2 Onions (finely chopped)
- 2-3 tbsp. Biryani Masala
- 1 ½ tsp. Salt
- 1 tsp. Red Chili Powder
- 2 tsp. Garam Masala
- 1/2 tsp. Turmeric
- 2 tsp. Coriander powder
- 1 tsp. Cumin whole
- 2 tbsp. Ghee/ Oil
- 1/2 cup hung Curd

FOR PREPARATION FOR PAKORA

Mix together all the ingredients for pakora's (dumpling) with some water. Heat oil in a heavy wok or pan. Make small balls using your palm and deep fry till golden brown. Drain on a kitchen towel. Keep aside

PREPARATION OF SOYA NUGGET

Heat ghee / oil in a pan add cumin and onions to it stir for a few mins, then add ginger garlic paste. Stir well add a few spoons of water if it is burning. Add the tomato puree and mix well. Now add chili powder, turmeric, coriander and then the soya nuggets cook for some time add half the methi pakora (dumpling). If water is less add more now add the biryani Masala curd and salt. Switch off the gas stove.

FOR PREPARATION OF RICE

Heat ghee or oil in a pan and add cumin along with the whole spices. Take enough water to boil the rice add salt. Now add rice when it is 85% done switch off the gas stove and strain the rice. Keep each grain separate, with the help of a fork.

TO ASSESMBLE

Grease an oven proof dish and spread half of the rice. Now cover with nutri soya. Mix a few of methi balls, then again rice and soya and a few of pakora. Spread the liquid on the rice and cover with fried onion. Set in oven for 15-20 min serve hot with raita and salan.

NUTRITIONAL VALUE (Approx)

Protein 13.9 g; Fat 5.5 g; Carbohydrate 101.7 g; Calories 512 cal (Per serving)

Roasted Eggplant Biryani

SERVING SIZE : 5-7

INGREDIENTS

- 1 large Eggplant (cut in 1" cubes)
- 3/4 cup hung Curd
- 2 tbsp. Gram flour / Besan
- 2 tbsp. Ginger Garlic paste
- 2 tbsp. Biryani Masala
- 1 tsp. Salt
- A pinch of Tandoori orange colour (Optional)
- 15-20 Mint Leaves fresh
- 2 Onion (finely chopped)
- 2 tbsp. Ghee / oil
- 1/2 tsp. Carom seeds (Ajwain)

INGREDIENTS FOR RICE

- 300 gm Basmati Rice (washed several times & soaked for 1.hr)
- 1 tbsp. Biryani Masala
- 2-3 pcs Brown Cardamom
- 3-4 Green Cardamom
- 3-4 Clove
- 6-7 Black Pepper
- 2 Bay Leaves
- 2" Cinnamon
- 1 tsp. Cumin whole
- 1 tbsp. Ghee / oil
- 1 tsp. Salt

INGREDIENTS FOR TOPPING

- 2-3 Onions (finely chopped) and fried in oil/ghee. Basil, Almonds and Cashew (fried or roasted).

FOR PREPARATION FOR RICE

Heat oil in a pan and then add cumin and the whole spices, add enough water to boil the rice, add salt. When the water boils add rice till it is 85% cooked, strain and keep aside.

MARINATION FOR PANEER

In a bowl take yogurt, all purpose flour, biryani masala, ginger, garlic paste, onions, salt, carom seeds, chilli powder and 2 tsp lemon juice. Combine very well. Gradually add the paneer pcs coat them with the marination, leave it for 30 minutes. Preheat the oven grease oven tray and spread the marinated paneer, keep the tray in the oven for 8-10 min, then toss sides of paneer let it be golden brown from both sides, switch off.

FOR TOMATO GRAVY

Fry the onions in ghee add tomato puree and spices, sugar, boil stirring for 6-8 min switch off the gas stove.

TO ASSEMBLE

Grease a bowl and spread rice layer then add few pcs of paneer and some of the tomato gravy. Then again rice, paneer and tomato gravy, add a few mint leaves fried onion. Finish with rice layer and sprinkle saffron milk. Sprinkle the fried onion and cashew. Bake in oven at 170 degree Celsius for 10-12 min before serving. Serve with tomato chutney and raita.

NUTRITIONAL VALUE (Approx)

Protein 15.0 g; Fat 6.9 g; Carbohydrate 42.7 g; Cholesterol 6.1 mg; Calories 290

Paneer Biryani

SERVING SIZE : 5-6

INGREDIENTS

- 400 gm Paneer (cut in 1 ½" cubes)
- 300 gm Basmati Rice (Washed & Soaked for 1-2 hrs)
- ½ cup Yogurt Thick
- 2 tbsp. Paste (green chili, garlic, ginger)
- 2-3 Onion (finely chopped)
- 1 tbsp. Biryani Masala
- 1 tsp. Salt
- 1/2 tsp. Red chili Powder
- 15-20 Mint Leaves
- 2 tsp. All purpose Flour or cornflour
- 1/2 tsp. Carom Seeds

FOR GRAVY

- 500 gm Tomato (Blanched peeled and pureed)
- 1 ½ tbsp. Biryani masala
- 1 tsp. Salt
- 1 tsp. Cumin Powder roasted
- 1 tsp. Sugar
- 1/2 tsp. Red Chili Powder
- 2 Onion chopped
- 1 tbsp. Ghee

INGREDIENTS FOR TOPPING

- 3-4 Onion (finely chopped and fried in oil or ghee)
- 10-12 Cashew (roasted or fried)
- Coriander fresh finely chopped
- 2-3 tbsp. Milk to soak Saffron
- 1/2 tsp green Cardamom Powder

FOR PREPARATION

Mix together hung curd, gram flour, ginger garlic paste, biryani masala, salt, tandoori colour (if using), onions carom seed and oil or ghee in a bowl. Add the eggplant pcs in the mixture and marinate for 1 hour. Heat the oven and spread the eggplant pcs on a greased tray keep the 10 to 12 min oven at 170 degree celsius. Then with the help of a spatula turn them around for the next side to roast. When done, switch off the oven. In a pan add ghee and cumin and all the whole spices stir on low flame till you can smell sweet aroma. Add 600 ml of water boil add salt. Then add rice and boil till they are nearly done, strain and keep aside. In a bowl mix 3/4 cup yogurt, salt, red chili powder, garam masala, biryani Masala. In 2-3 tbsp. milk soak saffron. Fry the onions till brown.

TO ASSEMBLE THE BIRYANI

Spread half the rice on the bottom of a greased dish. Then spread roasted eggplant. Followed by the yogurt mix, Cover it with the remaining rice. Now sprinkle the yogurt, saffron milk. Mint leaves and spread the fried onion on the rice and garnish with basil and coriander. Bake for 10-15 min. Serve hot with salan and Raita or any accompaniments of choice.

NUTRITIONAL VALUE (Approx)

Protein 15.0 g; Fat 6.9 g; Carbohydrate 42.7 g; Cholesterol 6.1 mg; Calories 290

Pulao & Kichri

1. Veg Pulao

2. Kashmiri Subaz Bahar Pulao

3. Baked Spicy Rice With Cheese

4. Assorted Dry Fruits Lemon Pulao

5. Tomato Rice (South Indian Style)

6. Vermicelli Pulao With Ginger and Veg

7. Coconut Curry With Rice

8. Chickpea Pulao

9. Punjab Mail

10. Patna Express (Lotus Stem Pulao)

11. Exotic Veg Pulao

12. Chana Dal Pulao

13. Bhutani Style Rice and Curry

14. Pumpkin and Pistachios Pulao

15. Khirchi Moth, Brown Rice and Dalia

16. Toor Dal Kichri

17. Sprout Whole Moong Kichri

18. South Style Kichri With Coconut

Veg Pulao

SERVING SIZE : 5-6

INGREDIENTS

- 2 ½ cup Rice (washed and soaked for 1 hour)
- 6 Cloves
- 6 Green Cardamom
- 6-8 Black Pepper
- 2 tsp. Cumin
- 2 Bay leaf
- 15-20 threads Saffron (soaked in 2 tbsp. milk)optional
- 1 Onion finely chopped
- 2 Potato cubes
- 1 tsp. Chat Masala
- 2-3 tbsp. Vegetable oil
- 30 gm Ginger grated
- 4-5 Garlic Clove minced
- 3 Tomato (Chopped and pureed)
- 3 tbsp. ground coriander (Dhania)
- 1 ½ tbsp. Cumin whole
- 1 tsp. Garam Masala
- 2 tsp. Biryani Masala
- 1 tsp. Chili Powder
- 1 Carrot (Finely Chopped)
- 300 gm Cauliflower (Cut in florets)
- 150 gm Mushroom halved (optional)
- 2/3 cup Yogurt Thick
- 2 handful Pea

FOR PREPARATION

Wash and soak rice for an hour. Boil enough water and add the rice along with the whole spices. When the rice is nearly 85% done switch off the gas stove and strain the rice. Keep aside.

FOR THE VEGETABLE

Heat oil in pan on medium flame when warm, add the onions fry for 3-4 minutes. Then add garlic ginger fry for 2-3 min add tomato puree along with ground coriander, cumin, chili powder, biryani masala, salt and pepper add the vegetables and stir. Add a little water, cook till the veggies are little tender add the yogurt (taste) to adjust the salt and spices add garam masala and switch off the gas stove.

TO ASSEMBLE

In a handi or oven proof dish spread the rice then the prepared vegetables. Sprinkle saffron milk if using, otherwise only chat masala and roasted cumin, bake in a preheated oven 160-170 Celsius for 8-10 minutes. Serve with accompaniments of choice.the rice- sprinkle milk with saffron. Garnish with coriander and fried onion bake for 20-25 min, serve hot with salan or tomato chutney and papad..

NUTRITIONAL VALUE (Approx)

Protein 4 g; Fat 7.3 g; Carbohydrate 37.4 g, Calories 231 cal

Kashmiri Subaz Bahar Pulao

SERVING SIZE : 5-6

INGREDIENTS FOR RICE COOKING

- 250 gm Basmati Rice (washed and soaked for 1hour)
- 1 tbsp. Ghee or mustard oil
- 6-7 Black Pepper whole
- 4-5 Cloves
- 3-4 Green Cardamoms
- 2" Cinnamon
- 1 tsp. whole Jeera (cumin)
- 2 Onion (finely chopped)
- 4-5 Garlic Clove minced
- 2" Ginger (finely grated)
- 1 ½ tsp. Salt

INGREDIENTS FOR THE VEGETABLE LAYER

- 200 gm Paneer (Cubed in 1" pcs and fried)
- 2 Stem of Lotus (cut in 1/4" round and boiled in salt water and strained)
- 100 gm boiled green Pea
- 3-4 Tomato (blanched and chopped without skin)
- 2 Onion (finely chopped)
- 3-4 Garlic Cloves minced
- 2 tbsp. Ghee/ Mustard oil
- 1" Ginger grated
- 1 ½ tsp. Garam masala
- 2 tsp. Biryani masala
- Salt to Taste

INGREDIENTS FOR TOPPING

- 3-4 Onion (finely chopped and fried)
- 1" Ginger grated
- 2 tbsp. Ghee
- 15-20 threads Saffron (Soaked in milk)
- 3/4 cup Dry fruits (walnut, cashew, almonds, raisin)
- 1 tsp. Salt
- 1/4 tsp. Pepper
- A pinch Chili Powder

FOR PREPARATION

In a pan add ghee and jeera (cumin) then the onion and garlic along with ginger and the other whole spices. When it is aromatic add the rice and water cook till rice is nearly done. Strain the rice, keep aside.

FOR THE VEGETABLE LAYER

Heat ghee in a pan and add the onion fry for 2-3 minutes. Now add the garlic and ginger stir with the onions for 2-3 minutes, keep the flame on medium. Now it is time to add tomato puree along with lotus stem, paneer and green peas. Add garam masala, biryani masala and salt when the liquid is nearly dry switch off the gas stove.

FOR TOP LAYER

Heat ghee and fry onion till crisp. Drain on a kitchen towel. Now add the dry fruits to the ghee and fry till aromatic transfer to a plate on a tissue so that extra ghee is soaked.

TO ASSEMBLE

In a heavy pan combine the prepared vegetables, and rice, toss very well add half the dry fruits. Transfer to a serving dish garnish with remaining dry fruits and serve.

NUTRITIONAL VALUE (Approx)

Protein 5.6 g; Fat 9.7 g; Carbohydrate 45.8 g; Calories 294 cal

Baked Spicy Rice With Cheese

SERVING SIZE : 4-6

INGREDIENTS

- 300 gm Basmati Rice (washed and soaked for 1 hour)
- 2 Bell Pepper (sliced in thin stripes)
- 2-3 Onions (chopped finely)
- 3-4 Garlic Cloves (minced)
- 3-4 Tomatoes (chopped)
- 1-2 Carrot (grated)
- 1 Spinach small bunch (chopped and washed)
- Salt to Taste
- 1/4 tsp. red Chili flake
- Black Pepper to taste
- 2-3 tbsp. oil
- 2-3 tbsp. Cheese grated if you want to use more go ahead

FOR PREPARATION

Heat oil in a pan, add onions fry them for 4 to 5 minutes. Add garlic bell pepper and carrots stir fry for 3 to 4 minutes. Add rice and tomato puree and 400 ml water. Add salt, pepper and give it a stir. When the rice is nearly done add the spinach and cheese give it a good stir. Switch off the gas stove. Transfer to a serving bowl sprinkle chilli flakes and some cheese, basil and coriander. Bake in a pre heated oven for 12 to 15 min on medium temperature. Serve hot

NUTRITIONAL VALUE (Approx)

Protein 18 g; Fat 11 g; Carbohydrate 58 g; Cholesterol 15 mg; Calories 255 cal

Assorted Dry Fruits Lemon Pulao

SERVING SIZE : 4-5

INGREDIENTS

- 350 gm Basmati Rice (washed and soaked for 1 hour)
- 3/4 cup mixed Dry fruit, almonds, cashew, walnuts, pistachios, fig
- 1-2 tbsp. Ghee or Olive oil
- 1 tsp. Cumin (roasted)
- 2-3 fresh Lemon leaves
- 1 tsp. Lemon Zest
- 1-2 tsp. Lemon juice
- 2 Onions (finely chopped)
- 2-3 Cloves garlic (minced)
- 1 tsp. Ginger (grated)
- 1/8 tsp. white Pepper ground
- Salt to taste
- 1/8 tsp black Pepper
- 2 Green chillies slit
- 1/3 tsp turmeric powder

FOR PREPARATION

In a pan heat oil or ghee. Add the onion fry for 3 to 4 minutes. Now add garlic and lemon zest and turmeric. Then add rice along with vegetable stock or water. Add salt pepper, stir occasionally. When done add pistachios mix well switch off the gas stove. Transfer to serving dish and serve accompanied with lemon pickle tomato chutney and yogurt

NUTRITIONAL VALUE(Approx)

250 calories, 120 gm carbohydrates, 11 gm protein.

Tomato Rice
(South Indian Style)

SERVING SIZE : 3-4

INGREDIENTS

- 200 gm Rice (washed and soaked for 1 hour)
- 2 tsp. Chana & Urad dal each (washed and soaked for 1 hr)
- 10-15 Curry leaves
- 1 green Chili slit
- 2 red dry Chili broken in small pieces
- 1-2 tbsp. Ghee / Butter
- 1 tbsp. Cashew roasted and broken in half
- 2 tbsp. Peanuts fried or roasted
- 2tbsp. Coriander powder
- 3-4 Tomatoes cut and liquidized in a mixer
- Salt and pepper to taste
- ½ tsp. garam masala
- 2 Onions chopped (Optional)
- 1 tsp. Jeera (cumin)
- 2 tbsp. fresh Coconut grated

FOR PREPARATION

In a pan heat on low flame add butter or ghee. Now add Onion and fry for 3 to 4 minutes. Add the red chilli and green chilli along with the chana and urad dal fry for a few minutes add curry leaves. Gradually add the the liquidized tomatoes salt, pepper and the rice. Add 1 ½ cup water and cook. Stir in between. When done garnish with peanuts, cashew, fresh grated coconut and coriander, serve hot.

NUTRITIONAL VALUE (Approx)

Protein 4.1 g; Fat 13.7 g; Carbohydrate 31.4 g; Calories 266

Vermicelli Pulao With Ginger and Veg

SERVING SIZE : 4-5

INGREDIENTS

- 200 gm Vermicelli dry roasted in pan until golden brown
- 150 gm French Beans (cut in ½" pcs)
- 2 Carrots grated
- 1"Ginger grated
- 1 Green Chili (finely chopped)
- 1 head Broccoli (6-8 florets)
- 1-2 Onions (finely chopped)
- 1 tbsp. Tomato Ketchup (Optional)
- 1-2 tbsp. Lemon Juice
- 1-2 tbsp. Oil/ Ghee
- Salt and Black pepper to taste
- 1/4 tsp. Red Chili powder
- 2 tbsp. Coriander leaves to garnish

FOR PREPARATION

In a pan add ghee or butter and fry the onions. Add green chillies and ginger. Then add Broccoli florets, carrots and french beans. When a little tender add the vermicelli, salt, pepper and chilli powder, add 1 cup of water stir well. When the vermicelli is soft and all the water is absorbed switch off the gas stove. Sprinkle lemon juice. Serve hot garnished with coriander leaves.

NUTRITIONAL VALUE (Approx)

Protein 5.5 g; Fat 3.6 g;
Carbohydrate 32.6 g; Calories 187

Coconut Curry With Rice

SERVING SIZE : 4-6

INGREDIENTS

- 300 gm Basmati Rice (washed and soaked for 1 hour)

FOR COCONUT CURRY

- 1 tbsp. Coriander Seeds whole
- 3-4 Red Dry Chilli
- 1/2 cup Onions chopped
- 1 tbsp. lemon Grass ground
- 3-4 garlic cloves minced
- 1 tsp. Salt
- 1 tsp. ginger grated
- 250 ml (Can) Coconut Milk
- 1 tsp. Curry powder
- 1 tsp. Sugar
- 4-6 Fresh Lemon leaves

FOR VEGETABLES

- 1 red Capsicum (cut in cubes)
- 1 Green Capsicum (cut in cubes)
- 4-6 Broccoli (broken in florets)
- 4-6 Cauliflower (broken in florets)
- 1 Carrot (sliced)
- 2 Onion (cut in med size)
- 1-2 tsp. Coconut oil
- Basil leaves for garnishing

FOR PREPARATION

Mix together all the ingredients for curry except coconut milk. Grind them in a mixer to a fine paste. In a heavy bottom pan heat oil and fry the onion for 2-3 minutes add the lemon leaves. Add the paste and stir fry on medium flame for a few minutes. Add the vegetables and. 1cup water and cook for 3-4 minutes. Now add the coconut milk, salt and sugar let it simmer for 4-5 minutes. In a separate pan boil water for rice. When it boils add salt and rice. Strain when done keep aside. In a shallow dish spread the boiled rice, make a well in the centre and pour the coconut curry. Serve garnished with basil leaves.

This combination is great as a meal refreshing as well tasteful with the goodness of vegetables and coconut milk.

NUTRITIONAL VALUE (Approx)

Protein 13.5 g; Fat 14.4 g; Carbohydrate 14.8 g; Cholesterol 24 mg; Calories 229.7 cal

Note

The vegetables used should crunchy or cook them 60% soft only.

Chickpea Pulao

SERVING SIZE : 6-7

INGREDIENTS

- 200 gm Chickpea (soaked over night then boiled with salt)
- 150 gm Rice Basmati (washed and soaked for 1 hr)
- 1 tbsp. Oil
- 1/4 tsp. Salt
- 1 large Onion
- 1 large Tomato (cubed)
- 3-4 garlic (minced)
- 1"ginger(grated)
- 3 tbsp. oil
- 1 tsp. Garam masala
- ¼ tsp. red Chili powder
- Salt and Pepper to Taste
- 2 tbsp Tomato Ketchup
- 1/2 tsp. baking Soda
- 1 ½ cup water

FOR PREPARATION

In a heavy bottom pan heat oil and saute the onions, add garlic and ginger. Now add garam masala, red pepper, black pepper. When the onion, ginger, garlic is aromatic. Add the cubed tomato, stir well. Add rice and enough water for the rice. When the rice is 80 % cooked add boiled chickpea. Cover the lid and lower the stove flame, let it cook for 5-7 minutes check in between. Add the tomato ketchup and stir with a fork. Serve hot garnished with grated paneer, coriander and crispy fried onions.

NUTRITIONAL VALUE (Approx)

Protein 6 g; Fat 8.5 g; Carbohydrate 37 g; Calories 243

Punjab Mail

SERVING SIZE : 6-7

INGREDIENTS

- 300 gm Jackfruit or Kathal (cut in small 1" pcs)
- 120 gm ghee (oil for frying)
- 2 -3 onions (finely chopped)
- 1/2 cup Hung Curd
- 3-4 green Cardamom
- 5 Cloves
- 1 ½ tsp. Salt
- 2 tsp. Poppy seeds (khas – khas)
- 2 tbsp Coriander (Dhania powder)
- 1 tsp. red Chilli powder
- 1 ½ tsp. Salt
- 2 Onions (finely chopped)
- 5-6 Kali mirch (Black Pepper)
- 1" Cinnamon
- 1 tsp. garam masala
- 2 tbsp. gram flour
- Coriander and Mint for garnishing
- 300 gm Basmati Rice (washed and soaked for 1 hour)

FOR PREPARATION

In a mixer jar take all the whole spices cardamom, cloves, poppy seeds, coriander, chilli, black pepper and onions grind to make a smooth paste. In a bowl mix together yogurt, gram flour, salt, and the paste mix very well till a smooth marination is ready. Now add fried kathal and coat very well with marination. Take another pan or a pressure cooker add some oil add cumin and onions and marinated kathal, stir for 4-5 min add water and rice with salt. Stir well. Fix the lid of cooker, when the whistle blows in 7 – 8 minutes, switch off the gas stove. Wait for pressure to drop, open the lid sprinkle garam masala, coriander and mint leaves and serve hot. The other way to make this is to prepare kathal masala separately and boiled rice on the side, garnish with fried onions carrots.

NUTRITIONAL VALUE (Approx)

Protein 10.5gm; Fat 17.2 gm;
Carbohydrate 41.7 gm; Calories 433

Patna Express
(Lotus Stem Pulao)

SERVING SIZE : 5-6

INGREDIENTS

- 250 gm Basmati rice soaked washed for 1 hour
- 4-5 green Cardamom
- 2-3 Cloves
- 3-4 Black Pepper whole
- 2 all Spice leaves or Bay leaf
- 1/2 tsp. red Chili powder
- 1½ tsp. Salt
- 250 gm Kamal Kakri (Lotus stem) peeled and cut in slices & boiled till tender
- 2-3 Tomatoes (cut in small cubes)
- 2 tsp. Curry powder
- 1/2 cup yogurt(Hung)
- 1 tsp. Salt
- 1 tsp. Cumin whole
- 2 tbsp. Ghee or oil
- 2 Onions sliced
- 3-4 tsp. Garlic Cloves minced (Optional)
- 1" Ginger grated
- 2 Green Chilli finely chopped
- 1 tsp. garam masala powder
- 2 tbsp. Coriander leaves (finely chopped)

FOR PREPARATION

In a heavy bottom pan heat oil and add the cumin, gradually add whole spices along with other spices and stir till it releases aroma. Then add ginger, garlic, green chilli and stir for 1-2 minutes. Now add the liquidized tomatoes with the curry powder, cook till a little thick. Then add the boiled lotus stem and let it simmer till it is well coated with tomato, yogurt, salt and red chilli. Now, add soaked rice and 2 cups of water. Stir lightly in between when rice is done switch off the gas stove. Keep covered for a few minutes. Garnish with fresh coriander finely chopped and serve with accompaniments of choice.

NUTRITIONAL VALUE (Approx)

Calories: 250 (Per serving)

Note

This rice and lotus stem pulao is very low in saturated Fat and cholesterol, it is also a good source of dietary, Fiber, Thiamin, Vitamin B6, Phosphorus, Potassium, Copper and Manganese, and a very good source of Vitamin C

Exotic Veg Pulao

SERVING SIZE : 5-6

INGREDIENTS

- 2 tbsp. oil
- 2 Onion (chopped)
- 2-3 garlic cloves (finely chopped)
- 1 green chilli (chopped)
- 2 long Egg plant (cut in 1''pcs)
- 15-20 French Beans (cut in 1" pcs)
- 1-2 Carrots (sliced)
- 300 gm Tomatoes (pureed)
- 120 gm Mushroom (sliced)
- 100 gm Paneer (cubed)
- 300 gm Basmati Rice (washed soaked for an hour)
- 1 red Capsicum (cut in cubes)
- 1"Ginger grated
- Coriander or mint to garnish

FOR PREPARATION

Heat oil in a heavy bottom pan. Add onion and cook for 2-3 minutes. When the onion is translucent then add garlic, green chilli and ginger cook for few minutes (3-4 min). Add the vegetables and stir. Now add rice and water or stock and tomatoes, cook till soft add the mushroom. When done top with paneer and serve garnished with coriander and tomato chutney.

NUTRITIONAL VALUE (Approx)

Protein 4 g; Fat 7.3 g; Carbohydrate 37.4 g; Cholesterol 0 mg; Calories 231 cal

Chana Dal Pulao

SERVING SIZE : 6-7

INGREDIENTS

- 200 gm Basmati rice (washed and soaked for 1 hour)
- 200 gm Chana Dal (washed and soaked for 2-3 hours)
- 1" Ginger grated
- 2 green chilli finely cut
- 2 tbsp. Ghee
- 1 ½ tsp. Cumin (Jeera)
- 1 large Carrot cut in cubes
- 100 gm Pea (shelled)
- 3-4 green Cardamom
- 3-4 Clove
- 3-4 Black Pepper
- 1 ½ tsp. Salt
- 1/2 tsp. Turmeric
- 1/2 tsp. Red chilli powder
- 1 tsp. garam masala
- 2 tbsp. Coriander leaves chopped
- 1 tsp. Cumin roasted

FOR PREPARATION

In a heavy bottom pan heat half of the ghee add cumin, clove black pepper, green chilli, ginger, turmeric stir well. Add chana dal along with salt. Now add water stir well and let it cook for 5-6 min. Add rice and vegetables. Cook till the rice and dal is tender not mushy, add garam masala. Switch off the gas stove. Sprinkle roasted cumin and coriander. Serve hot with accompaniments of choice.

NUTRITIONAL VALUE (Approx)

Protein 16.3 g; Fat 21.2 g; Carbohydrate 63.3 g; Calories 330

Bhutani Style Rice and Curry

SERVING SIZE : 5-6

INGREDIENTS

- 150 gm Red Rice (washed and soaked for 2 hours or more)
- 100 gm Basmati Rice (washed and soaked for 1-2 hours)
- 1 ½ tsp. Salt
- 3-4 green Chilli slit
- 2 tbsp. Vegetable oil/ Olive Oil
- 1 long eggplant cut in cubes
- 15 0 gm Cauliflower (broken in small florets)
- 1-2 Carrot (finely sliced)
- 2-3 pcs Onions (sliced)
- 2-3 Cheese cubes (grated)
- 1 cup Milk
- 1 cup water
- 3-4 Lemon grass (stalk white part)
- 1 tsp. Salt
- 1/4 tsp. Black pepper (ground)

FOR PREPARATION

In a pan boil water add salt and then red rice, boil till tender 12-15 minutes. When done strain and keep aside. In the same pan boil basmati white rice with salt. When done strain keep aside

FOR THE CURRY

In a heavy pan heat oil and add onion and fry for 3-4 minutes. Make a bunch of lemon grass add in the onion and stir fry. Now add green chillies, water and other vegetables. Cook till tender, now add salt, black pepper and milk, add cheese and mix well. After the cheese has melted and become creamy. Check if it is thick add 1/2 cup water switch off the gas stove. Take out the lemon grass bunch and serve the hot curry accompanied with mixed red and white rice.

NUTRITIONAL VALUE (Approx)

Calories 350; Protein 8.9 g; Fat 14.9 g; Carbohydrate 50.4 g

Pumpkin and Pistachios Pulao

SERVING SIZE : 4-6

INGREDIENTS

- 300 gm Basmati Rice (washed and soaked for 1 hour)
- 500 gm pumpkin (peeled and cut in 3/4 " cubes)
- Grease a tray and spread pumpkin pcs, sprinkle, salt, pepper and oil and bake for 10-12 minutes in a pre heated oven at 170 degrees C
- 1 tsp. Cumin
- 2 tbsp. Ghee or olive oil
- 2 Onion (finely chopped)
- 3-4 clove garlic minced (optional)
- 1" ginger grated
- 2 tsp. fennel seeds whole (Sabut Saunf)
- 1/8 tsp. Nut meg powder
- 80 gm roasted Pistachios (coarsely broken)
- 1/2 tsp. cinnamon powder
- 1/4 tsp. red chilli powder
- 1/4 tsp. black pepper
- Salt to taste
- Coriander and Parsley for garnishing

FOR PREPARATION

Heat oil in a heavy bottom pan add cumin, ginger, onion, garlic, one by one and saute stirring well. Now add rice and cook till 80% done. Add the roasted pumpkin pcs along with the fennel and spices. Mix well with a fork, if the water has evaporated totally and the rice is not done add a little more water. Switch of the gas stove. Sprinkle the pistachios and a pinch of nutmeg. Garnish with coriander or parsley serve hot with accompaniments.

Khirchi Moth, Brown Rice and Dalia

SERVING SIZE : 4-6

INGREDIENTS

- 100 gm moth or moong split (washed and soaked for 1 hr)
- 75 gm brown rice (washed and soaked for 1 hrs)
- 100 gm broken wheat or dalia lightly roasted
- 100 gm pumpkin cubed in small pcs
- 100 gm cabbage
- 100 gm beans
- 1 tbsp. ghee
- ¼ tsp. turmeric
- Salt and pepper to taste
- ½ tsp. garam masala
- 1 onion (optional) finely chopped
- 1 tsp. cumin
- 1" Ginger grated
- A pinch Hing (Asafetida)

FOR PREPARATION

In a heavy pan heat ghee add cumin, asafetida, and ginger gradually add brown rice and moth along with dalia or broken wheat. Stir for 2-3 min add 2 cups water, dalia and dal. Stir and cook again till a creamy consistency is achieved switch off the gas stove. Sprinkle ghee on top along with garam masala. Serve hot with tomato chutney and yogurt.

Toor Dal Kichri

SERVING SIZE : 6-7

INGREDIENTS

- 1 cup Rice (washed and soaked for 1 hour)
- 3/4 cup Toor Dal (washed and soaked for 1 hour)
- 1" pcs Ginger (grated)
- 5-6 Curry Leaves
- 2 green Chilli slit
- 2 Bay leaves
- 2-3 tbsp. Ghee
- 1 tsp. Mustard seeds
- 1 tsp. Cumin seeds raw
- 1 tsp. roasted Cumin powder
- 1/2 tsp. Red Chilli powder
- 1/2 tsp. Turmeric
- 1 ½ tsp.   Salt
- 2 Onions finely chopped and fried in ghee (Optional)
- 2 dry Red Chilli

FOR PREPARATION

In a heavy bottom pan heat 1 tbsp ghee add cumin, mustard, bay leaves, curry leaves, green chilli and ginger. When they splutter add the rice and dal and 3 ½ cup water. Add turmeric, chilli and salt cover and cook on low flame till soft but not mushy. Heat ghee in a small pan add the red dry chilli fry till crisp transfer to the bowl of khichri if using onion spread on the bowl and serve hot with Raita chutney, paped, and mango pickle.

NUTRITIONAL VALUE (Approx)

Calories 130; Carbohydrates 11.5, Protein 3 gm

Sprout Whole Moong Kichri

SERVING SIZE : 6-7

INGREDIENTS

- 200 gm Green Whole Moong (sprouted)
- 200 gm Rice (washed and soaked 1 hr)
- 1 tbsp. ginger paste
- 1 tbsp. Ghee
- 1 tsp. cumin/ raw whole
- 2-3 Brown Cardamom
- 2-3 Onion finely chopped and fried (Optional)
- 1 Zucchini or bottle gourd (lauki) cut in cubes
- 150 gm Sweet Corn
- Salt and black pepper to taste
- 1 tsp. Roasted Cumin ground
- 1 tsp. Garam Masala
- 1 tsp. Turmeric
- Mint or Coriander to garnish

FOR PREPARATION

In a pan or pressure cooker heat ghee add cumin stir till it is golden then add turmeric, ginger paste and fry. Add 250 ml. water. Then add the moong and rice, and all vegetables. Along with salt & black pepper, simmer on low flame. Add more water and let it cook for 15-20 minutes on low flame or till the moong is soft. Switch off the gas stove. Sprinkle garam masala and fried onions if using. Add ghee and serve hot with combination of tomato chutney and raita.

NUTRITIONAL VALUE (Approx)

Protein 5.2 g; Fat 9.1 g;
Carbohydrate 32.2 g; Calories 231

South Style Kichri With Coconut

SERVING SIZE : 3-4

INGREDIENTS

- 200 gm Basmati Rice (washed and soaked for 1 hr)
- 150 gm red Moth (Lentil) washed and soaked for 1 hr
- 2-3 large Carrots (peeled and coarsely grated.)
- 1 cup fresh Coconut (grated)
- 1-2 green chillies slit
- 1" Ginger (grated)
- 2-3 brown Cardamom
- 1 tbsp. Ghee
- 2 onions (thinly sliced and fried in ghee)
- 1 ½ tsp. cumin whole
- 1/2 tsp. Black Pepper
- 1 ½ tsp. Salt
- Fresh Mint leaves to garnish

FOR PREPARATION

In a heavy bottom pan heat ghee and add cumin, cardamom, bay leaves and stir till aromatic. Add green chillies and ginger and cook for 1-2 minutes. Add rice and 400 ml water along with salt when half done add carrot and half the coconut cook till done. Switch off the gas stove and sprinkle mint, onions and coconut, serve hot with accompaniments.

Risotto & Quinoa

Kidney Bean Risotto

SERVING SIZE : 7-8

INGREDIENTS

- 300 gm Kidney Beans (soaked and boiled with salt till 85% done)
- 2 tbsp. Olive Oil
- 2 onions (finely chopped)
- 3-4 Garlic cloves minced
- 200 gm Brown Rice / Arborio Rice
- 300 ml vegetable stock
- 300 ml Water
- Salt to Taste
- Pepper to Taste
- 1 Red Bell Pepper finely chopped
- 250 gm Mushroom quartered
- 50 gm Cashew roasted or fried
- 2-3 tbsp. Cheese grated
- 2 tbsp. Coriander Leaves chopped

FOR PREPARATION

Heat 1/2 the oil in large heavy pan. Add onion and cook stirring well for 4-5 minutes until soft. Add garlic and cook. Add rice and stir for 2 minutes till the rice is coated with oil. Add stock and salt and bring to boil reduce the heat and cover the pan. Simmer for 5-30 minutes till liquid has been absorbed.

Heat the oil in a separate pan add bell pepper and cook 5 minutes add mushroom, garlic and cook 4-5 minutes. Stir the rice into the skillet, add the beans parsley and cashew season with salt and pepper stir well. Transfer to a serving dish sprinkle coriander, cashew and cheese. Serve hot with coriander.

NUTRITIONAL VALUE (Approx)

Protein 16.3 g; Fat 21.2 g;
Carbohydrate 43 g; Calories 329.6 cal

Indian Style Risotto

SERVING SIZE : 4-6

INGREDIENTS

- 1 tsp. Ghee or oil
- 1 tsp. Jalapenos or green chilli
- 1 tsp. Cumin
- 1 cup yellow Moong soaked
- 1/8 tsp.(hing) Asatoefida
- 1 ½ cup Arborio Rice wiped with a kitchen towel
- 1 Cauliflower (cut in florets)
- 6 cup Water or stock
- 1/2 tsp. Turmeric
- 1 ½ tsp. Salt
- 1/2 cup Pea shelled
- Black Pepper to Taste
- 1 tbsp. Coriander powder(Dhania)
- 1 Onion chopped
- 2-3 tbsp. cheese grated (optional)

FOR PREPARATION

Heat ghee in a pan add cumin, hing, onion and jalapenos fry till onion is translucent. Add the rice and stir well for 4-5 minutes or till the color changes. Add turmeric, salt, pepper, pea and cauliflower, add 2 cups of water. Then add moong dal and add 2 cups of water let it simmer on medium flame, stirring in between, add more water if required. When it is soft and mushy switch off the gas stove. Garnish with roasted cumin and coriander leaves.

NUTRITIONAL VALUE (Approx)

Protein 8.0 g; Fat 7.8 g; Carbohydrate 33.5 g; Cholesterol 7.5 mg; Calories 220.2 cal

Note
Unique combination of Arborio rice and moong dal with vegetables gives a creamy texture.

Baked Quinoa With Veggies

SERVING SIZE : 3-4

FOR QUINOA

- 1 cup Quinoa (soaked for 1 hour after rinsing in it 2 cup water)
- 1 tsp. Salt
- 1 tsp. Curry Powder

FOR VEGGIES

- 2 Carrot (finely chopped)
- 12-15 French Beans chopped
- 1 Capsicum finely chopped
- 2-3 Onions chopped
- 1 Green Chilli finely chopped
- 1 tsp. Ginger grated
- 3-4 Tomatoes puree
- Olive oil / Vegetable
- 2 tsp. oil or Ghee
- Salt to Taste
- 1/4 tsp. Black Pepper
- 1 tsp. roasted Cumin Powder (Jeera)
- 1-2 tsp. Ketchup (Optional)
- 1-2 Amul Cheese cubes grated

FOR PREPARATION

In a pan boil the quinoa with salt and curry powder about 10-12 minutes. When the water evaporates and quinoa is soft and firm switch off the gas stove. Heat a heavy pan add oil or ghee, add the onions stir for a few minutes (3-4 min.), add ginger and green chilli stir again. Add vegetables and mix, cook for a few minutes. Now, add the quinoa and tomatoes puree along with salt and 1/2 cup water cook for 3-4 minutes. Switch off the gas stove mix the ketchup now. Transfer to a bowl and spread grated cheese on top, bake in a pre heated oven at 180 degree for 10-12 minutes and serve hot.

NUTRITIONAL VALUE (Approx)

Protein 13.5 g; Fat 8.4g; Carbohydrate 55.1 g; Calories 242 cal

Pongal

SERVING SIZE : 3-4

INGREDIENTS

- 150 gm Basmati Rice (soaked)
- 125 gm Moong dal (soaked)
- 2 tbsp. Ghee
- 1/2 cup Cashew (roasted)
- 1 tsp. Cumin raw
- 1 tsp. Cumin roasted
- 1 pinch Asafoetida (hing) ground
- 2-3 Onion sliced and fried in ghee
- 8-10 Curry leaves
- 2 tbsp. Coconut grated
- Salt to taste
- 1/2 tsp. Turmeric
- 1 cup vegetables Pea Carrot etc (optional)

FOR PREPARATION

In a pressure cooker heat 1 tbsp. ghee add cumin and hing. When it crackles add curry leaves, rice and dal, vegetables and 2 ½ to 3 cup water, along with salt and turmeric. Put the lid and wait for 2 whistle. Switch off the gas stove. Wait for the pressure to drop. Transfer to a serving bowl sprinkle the roasted cumin, fried onions, cashew and coconut. Serve hot with coconut chutney and yogurt.

NUTRITIONAL VALUE (Approx)

Calories 214; Carbohydrates 23 g, Protein 4-8 gm

Sweets

Nuts and Coconut Balls

SERVING SIZE : 4-5

INGREDIENTS

- 15-20 dates deseeded and chopped
- 2 tbsp. peanuts dry roasted
- 15-20 cashews roasted
- 10-15 almonds coarsely ground
- 2 tbsp. Sunflower seeds
- 2 tbsp. Pumpkin seeds
- 1 cup desiccated coconut
- 2 tbsp. honey or Jaggery syrup

make paste
In mixer

Coarsely
Ground

FOR PREPARATION

In date and peanut paste add the almonds, cashew, sunflower, pumpkin seeds and half the coconut. If more binding in needed add, Jaggery syrup or honey, make small balls and roll in desiccated coconut and serve.

NUTRITIONAL VALUE (Approx)

Calories 80; Fiber 27 gm; Protein 18 gm; Carbohydrates 65 gm

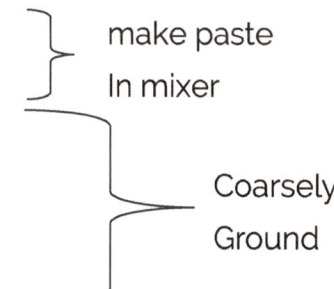

Note

These nut and coconuts balls are sugar free and high in nutrition. Nuts keep you full for a long time.

Guava Ice Cream

SERVING SIZE : 8-10

INGREDIENTS

- 2 Guava freshly grated without seeds
- 400 ml coconut milk thick
- 200 ml. cream thick
- 400 ml guava juice (Real or any other)
- 100 ml. condensed milk or 1/4 cup sugar
- Few drops of green colour (optional)

FOR PREPARATION

In a bowl add guava juice, condensed milk, cream and coconut milk. If not using condensed milk replace with sugar, mix with a blender very well. Add colour if using and half of the grated guava. Set in the freezer for 2 hrs. Whisk it with fork or mix lightly with the blender. Set again in the freezer and let it set for a few hours.

The unique taste of guava ice cream with coconut is very tasteful and soothing.

NUTRITIONAL VALUE (Approx)

Calories 286; Carbohydrates 28 gm

Baked Paneer Sweet

SERVING SIZE : 8-10

INGREDIENTS

- 300 gm fresh paneer grated and smoothen with palm for a few minutes (8-10 minutes)
- 200 gm hung curd
- 200 gm condensed milk
- 1/4 tsp. Cardamom powder
- 2 tbsp. almonds peeled and finely chopped
- 1tbsp. Pista (Pistachios) finely chopped
- 10-15 strands of saffron soaked in milk

FOR PREPARATION

Mix together paneer, curd, condensed milk very well add cardamom powder transfer to a baking dish sprinkle, almonds and Pista and spread the saffron milk. Bake in a pre heated oven for 12-15 minutes. Let it cool down to room temperature and serve.

NUTRITIONAL VALUE (Approx)

Calories 275

Orange Carrot Sweet Rice

SERVING SIZE : 8-10

INGREDIENTS

- 3 Orange (save the peel)
- 100 gm Sugar
- 3 tbsp. Ghee or Butter
- 100 gm mixed Nuts (or even more)
- 300 gm Rice long grain
- 4-5 grated Carrots
- 1/4 cup milk
- 1 tbsp. milk & saffron strand
- 1/2 tsp Salt

FOR PREPARATION

In a pan boil 2 cup water add 2 tsp sugar and boil the orange peel for 8 to 10 min. Change the water and again boil peels with more sugar till the bitterness has gone. Boil water with ½ tsp salt add the rice, boil till done strain and keep aside. In a heavy bottom pan add ghee or butter add the grated carrots and orange peels, also add sugar. Stir well add saffron milk and ¼ cup milk. Let it simmer till the liquid dries up add the boiled rice mix half the dry fruits. Transfer to a serving dish garnish with remaining dry fruits and orange segments. Serve hot.

NUTRITIONAL VALUE (Approx)

Calories: 325

Note

The aroma of orange peels the sweetness and color of carrots is attractive.

Orange Fussion

SERVING SIZE : 8-9

INGREDIENTS

- 3-4 Orange segments separated
- 1 Lt. Orange Juice (Real or any other)
- 3-4 tsp. Corn flour
- 1/4 can Coconut milk
- 1/2 can Condensed milk
- 2 tbsp. Lemon Juice
- 1 tbsp. Orange zest
- 1 cup Heavy cream (optional)

FOR PREPARATION

Boil the orange juice in a heavy pan. Save some juice to m ix corn flour. When the juice is about to boil add the juice mixed with corn flour and stir well add the condensed milk and coconut milk. Switch off the gas add lemon juice and orange zest, stir well and cool. Set in a freezer (1 Hour). Then keep in fridge. Garnish with orange segments and mint leaves.

NUTRITIONAL VALUE (Approx)

Protein 1.23 g; Fat 0.16 g;
Carbohydrate 15.39 g; Calories 220 cal

Mango Tiramisu

SERVING SIZE : 5-6

INGREDIENTS

- 1 cup Mango juice or pulp (in season)
- 3/4 cup Coconut Milk
- 1 tsp. Rice Flour
- 2 tsp. Custard powder
- 2 tbsp. Sugar
- 1/2 tsp. Lemon Juice
- Coffee powder for dipping
- Mango for garnishing
- 6-8 ginger biscuits

FOR PREPARATION

Boil 3/4 of the mango juice. Add custard powder mixed in 1/4 cup of the remaining mango juice and add to the boiling juice. When it becomes thick, switch off the gas stove. Let it cool. Boil the coconut milk, rice flour and sugar to form a thick coat add the lemon juice. Boil ½ cup water. Add 2 tsp coffee powder and 2 tsp sugar. In individual glass bowls, spread the coconut mixture then biscuit dipped in coffee liquid then spoon some mango sauce again layer with biscuit and some coconut and mango sauce. Garnish with mango slice, chocolate shavings and mint. Refrigerate for 2-3 hours before serving.

2 Layers Chocolate Rice Souffle

SERVING SIZE : 5-6

INGREDIENTS

For 1 Layer Chocolate

- 1 cup milk + 1/4 cup
- 3 Tsp. Rice flour or 2 tsp. corn flour
- 4 Tsp. Sugar
- 3 Tsp. Coco powder or 1/2 cup Chocolate chips
- 1 Tsp. Vanilla essences

For 2 Layer Chocolate

- 3 Tbsp. Sugar
- 1 cup milk
- 3 Tsp. Rice Flour or Corn flour
- Chocolate sauce and strawberry sauce to garnish or chocolate shavings or fresh strawberry sliced.

FOR PREPARATION

In a heavy pan heat 1 cup of milk add sugar. In remaining ¼ cup add rice flour or corn flour, coco powder or chocolate chips and mix well before adding to the boiling milk stir continuously till thick add vanilla essences and switch off the gas stove. Let it cool stirring well. Transfer to a small square glass bowl. In another pan add sugar and let it caramelize then add the milk mixed with corn flour or rice flour and stir well to form a thick sauce. Stir to cool then spread evenly over the coco sauce in the bowl. Cool in fridge for some time and then garnish with Hershey's chocolate sauce or strawberry sauce, chocolate shavings and fresh sliced strawberry.

Rice Pudding

SERVING SIZE : 5-6

INGREDIENTS

- 1 Tbsp. of ghee or butter
- 80 gm rice washed and soaked
- 750 ml milk
- 3 tbsp. / 60 gm Sugar
- 2 tbsp. Brown Sugar
- 125 gm dry fruits, pistachios, raisins, almonds, roughly chopped
- 1/4 tsp. Cardamom powder
- A pinch of cinnamon and nutmeg

FOR PREPARATION

In a heavy bottom pan boil milk and add the soaked rice. Stir and cook on med flame till the rice is soft and creamy. Add the sugar and half of the ghee or butter. Grease a baking dish with butter or ghee and transfer the rice pudding. Garnish with dry fruits and bake in a pre heated oven 160 degree for 15-18 minutes till golden on top. Cool in the refrigerator and serve.

Raita

1. Palak Raita

2. Cucumber Walnut Raita

3. Kachumber Raita

4. Fried Bhindi (Okra) Raita

5. Crispy Spinach Raita

6. Carrot Peanut Raita

7. Mixed Vegetable and Boondi Raita

Palak Raita

SERVING SIZE : 3-4

INGREDIENTS

- 200 gm Spinach (finely chopped and steamed)
- 1 Carrot (grated)
- 400 gm Yogurt (Strained)
- 1 tsp. Sugar
- 3/4 tsp. Salt
- 1/4 tsp. Pepper
- 3/4 tsp. Cummin Powder

FOR PREPARATION

Extract the extra water from the steamed spinach. Mix the sugar, Salt, Cummin Powder, Pepper in yogurt and add the Spinach and carrot and mix well, In case it is very thick add few spoons of milk. Cool and serve garnished with Coriander leaves and Cummin powder.

Cucumber Walnut Raita

SERVING SIZE : 3-4

INGREDIENTS

- 300 gm Yogurt
- 1 Cucumber (seeded and finely chopped or grated)
- 1 Clove garlic (finely minced)
- 1/2 tsp. Ginger grated
- 8-10 Walnuts finely chopped
- 1 tsp. Cumin Powder
- A pinch red Chili Powder
- 1 tbsp. Coriander leaves (finely chopped)
- Salt and Pepper to Taste

FOR PREPARATION

Smoothen the yogurt with a whisk add the spices then ginger, garlic coriander and cucumber serve cold with a dash of cumin.

Kachumber Raita

SERVING SIZE : 3-4

INGREDIENTS

- 1 Cucumber grated
- 1 Carrot grated
- 1 Boiled Potato (cut in small pcs)
- 1 Onion (finely chopped)
- 1 Green Chili (finely chopped)
- 1 bunch Coriander leaves (chopped)
- 300 gm Yogurt
- ½ tsp.Cumin
- ½ tsp. Salt
- ½ tsp. Pepper

FOR PREPARATION

Mix together all the vegetables smoothen the yogurt with a whisk add the vegetables, Salt, Cumin and pepper and mix well. Cool and serve garnished with coriander leaves.

Fried Bhindi (Okra) Raita

SERVING SIZE : 3-4

INGREDIENTS

- 200 gm Okra (Bhindi) washed, dried and cut 1/2" pcs.
- 2tbsp Gram Flour
- 300 gm Yogurt (strained)
- 1/2 tsp Salt
- 1/2 tsp. Cumin (roasted)
- 1/4 tsp Black pepper
- 1/2 tsp Red Chili powder
- Oil for frying Bhindi

FOR PREPARATION

Heat oil in a pan. In a bowl mix gram flour, salt, chilli powder add water and make a smooth batter, rest it for a few minutes. When the oil is hot coat the cut Bhindi in the batter and fry in hot oil till crispy. Spread on a paper towel so that the extra oil is soaked. In the strained yogurt add salt, cumin, black pepper, chili powder mix well and add the fried Bhindi when ready to serve. It is optional to cut Bhindi ½" or any size even slit lengthwise can be used.

Crispy Spinach Raita

SERVING SIZE : 3-4

INGREDIENTS

- 10-15 fresh spinach(washed and strained)
- 2-3 tbsp gram flour (Besan)
- 1 tsp Salt
- 1 tsp Red Chili powder
- 1/2 tsp Cumin powder
- 300 gm Yogurt powder (strained)
- 1 tbsp green chutney
- 1 tsp Sugar
- 2 tsp Pomegranate to garnish
- Oil for frying

FOR PREPARATION

Mix together the gram flour salt red chili and cumin add water to make a consistent batter. Now, heat oil in a pan and fry the spinach dipped in gram flour batter till crisp, drain and spread on a paper towel. Mix salt, chilli powder, cumin and sugar in yogurt. Just before serving place the crispy spinach in a serving dish pour the yogurt and serve immediately garnished with green chutney and pomegranate.

Carrot Peanut Raita

SERVING SIZE : 3-4

INGREDIENTS

- 300 gm Yogurt (Hung curd)
- 2 pc Carrots (grated and boiled 4-5 minutes)
- 1 Ginger (grated)
- 1 Green Chili (finely chopped)
- 1/4 cup Coriander leaves (finely chopped)
- 2 tbsp roasted Peanuts(finely chopped)
- 1 tsp Cumin powder
- 1/2 tsp Red chilli powder
- 1 tsp Salt

FOR PREPARATION

Whisk the Yogurt add Salt, Red chili powder, Ginger, Green chili, Carrot, Peanuts and Coriander (Save Same for Garnish) cool and serve.

Raita

Mixed Vegetable and Boondi Raita

SERVING SIZE : 3-4

INGREDIENTS

- 300 gm Yogurt whisked
- 1 Cucumber(finely chopped)
- 1/2 tsp Black pepper
- 1/4 tsp Red chilli powder
- 1/4 tsp Cumin powder roasted
- 1 boiled Potato(finely cubed)
- 1 Tomato(deseeded and cubed)
- 1/2 cup Boondi (crispy fried beads of gram folour)
- 1 tbsp fresh Coriander(finely chopped)
- 1 tsp Sugar
- 1tsp Salt

FOR PREPARATION

In the whisked yogurt add salt, pepper, chili powder, cumin and sugar. Add the finely chopped vegetables and boondi mix well. Garnish with fresh coriander and a dash of cumin. Serve with Pulao or Biryani.

Accompaniments

1. Baked Potatoes With Fennel

2. Beans and Pumpkin Stew

3. Mirchi Ka Salan

4. Tomato Chutney

5. Ginger Cranberry Chutney

6. Onion Cutney

7. Green Chutney

8. Zatar

Baked Potatoes With Fennel

SERVING SIZE : 5-6

INGREDIENTS

- 700 gm Potatoes washed and sliced in thin rounds
- 2-3 tbsp. Butter
- 2 Onions sliced
- 1 ½ tbsp. Fennel leaves chopped fine
- 200 ml milk
- 50 gm. Cheese grated
- 150 ml. cream (optional)
- 1 ½ tbsp. all purpose flour
- 1 tbsp. Olive oil
- 1/4 tsp. pepper
- Salt to taste
- 1 tsp. thyme fresh or dried

FOR PREPARATION

Boil water and add the potatoes slices in it. Boil for a few minutes then strain. Add olive oil and separate with a fork. In a pan heat half of the butter and fry the onions for 4-5 minutes. Mix the milk with flour and add to the onion when the sauce consistency is ready add salt and pepper and half of the cheese, add potato and stir, transfer to a baking dish garnish with fennel leaves and thyme add the remaining cheese bake in a pre heated oven for 40-45 minutes. Sprinkle some red chili powder for colour and serve hot.

NUTRITIONAL VALUE (Approx)

Calories 160

Beans and Pumpkin Stew

SERVING SIZE : 5-6

INGREDIENTS

- 1 Onion finely chopped
- 2 Garlic minced
- 4 Tomatoes cubed
- 1 tsp Paprika
- ½ tsp. Cumin
- 1 cup white Beans (Lobhia) soaked for 4 hr & boiled till soft
- 1 can sweet corn (200 gm)
- 250 gm Pumpkin (cubed)
- 2 tbsp. Basil (fresh)
- 2 tbsp. Oil
- Salt and pepper to taste

FOR PREPARATION

Saute onions in a heavy bottom pan with some oil add garlic, tomato, paprika and cumin, cook for 2 to 3 minutes. Then add beans and sweet corn. Now add pumpkin and little water or milk. Then lightly mash the vegetables. Cover and cook over low heat, till done, switch off the gas stove. Spread basil leaves roughly torn and serve with rice or potato.

NUTRITIONAL VALUE (Approx)

Protein 23 g; Fat 1.6 g; Carbohydrate 46 g; Calories 290 cal

Mirchi Ka Salan

SERVING SIZE : 5-6

INGREDIENTS

- 15-20 Green Chilies
- 2 tbsp. Mustard oil or (Til) Sesame oil
- 3-4 Red chilies dry
- 1/2 cup Peanuts roasted
- 2 tsp. Mustard seeds
- 1 ½ tbsp. Coriander whole seeds
- 1 tsp. Turmeric powder
- 2 tbsp. Garlic Ginger paste
- 2 Onions (finely chopped)
- 2 tbsp. Coconut grated (optional)
- 2-3 tbsp. Sesame seeds
- 15-20 Curry leaves
- 100 gm tamarind
- 2-3 tbsp. Jaggery
- Salt to taste
- Oil for Frying

FOR PREPARATION

Soak the tamarind and jaggery in 300 ml water for 1 hour. Heat oil, wipe the chilies with kitchen towel and slit. Heat oil fry the green chillies and keep them on a paper towel. In a heavy pan dry roast all the spices peanuts and coconut. Cool and grind in a mixer. Heat oil and add cumin, curry leaves, onion and sauté, add the ginger garlic paste, add ground masala stir for 5-7 min. Add water to get the right consistency. Add turmeric powder, Jaggery tamarind paste, lastly add the fried chilies and salt simmer on low flame for 10-12 min. Serve hot with Biryani or pulao and even roti.

Instead of chillies, fried eggplant, mixed vegetables like cauliflower and carrots or even fried (arbi) colocasia can be replaced.

NUTRITIONAL VALUE (Approx)

Calories 143, Carbohydrates 9.2 gm, Fat 11.3 gm

Tomato Chutney

INGREDIENTS

- 300 gm Tomato skinned and chopped or pureed
- 2 Red dry chilli broken
- 1 tsp Dhania (dry whole)
- 1 tsp Jeera (cumin)
- 1 tsp Salt.
- 1/4 Pepper
- 100 gm Jaggery
- 1 tbsp oil
- ¼ cup vinegar white

FOR PREPARATION

In a pan heat oil add cumin, dhania and red chilli. Then add jaggery, tomato, salt and pepper. Let it simmer till a little thick, switch off the gas flame and let it cool.

NUTRITIONAL VALUE (Approx)

Calories 143, Carbohydrates 9.2 gm, Fat 11.3 gm

Ginger Cranberry Chutney

INGREDIENTS

- 200 gm Cranberry (soaked in 1 cup water)
- 8 to 10 dates deseeded and soaked in water
- 2 tbsp ginger grated
- 1/4 tsp cinnamon power
- 1 tsp salt
- 1/8 tsp black pepper
- 1/2 tsp red chilli powder

FOR PREPARATION

Boil 1/2 cup water and all the ingredients and let it simmer for 20 minutes. When it is mushy and soft switch off the gas stove. Let it cool then serve.

Onion Chutney

INGREDIENTS

- 300 gm small onions
- 2 tbsp tamarind paste
- 2 tbsp honey or brown sugar
- 2-3 tbsp olive oil
- 1 tsp salt
- 3/4 red chilli powder
- 1 tsp chilli flakes
- 1 small bunch fresh Coriander
- 3-4 garlic minced

FOR PREPARATION

Heat oil fry the onions and garlic till golden brown. Add tamarind paste, salt and red chilli, honey or brown sugar and cook a few minutes. Then add coriander and switch off the gas stove. Cool and coarsely grind in a mixer jar and store in a air tight jar.

Green Chutney

INGREDIENTS

- 25-30 curry leaves
- 25-30 mint leaves
- 150 gm coriander fresh, washed and chopped finely
- 2 green chillies chopped
- 1 small raw mango grated (if not available 1 tsp of amchur)
- Salt, 1 tsp sugar or Jaggery
- 1 tbsp yogurt
- 2 tsp lemon juice

FOR PREPARATION

Mix all ingredients in the mixer jar with little water or curd and grind it to a smooth paste.

Accompaniments for kichri, pulao, biryanis and fried spinach raita etc.

Zatar

Zatar is a Mediterranean spice for salad etc. Its Ingredients are:-

INGREDIENTS

- 7-8 tbsp. Thyme dried
- 2 tsp. Marjoram dried
- 3-4 tsp. Sesame seeds roasted
- 2 tsp. sumac (Indian amchur can be used)
- 1 tsp. salt
- Powder all together and sprinkle on salad as needed, store the rest in a glass jar

RICE VARIETIES

NOTES:

1. Brown Rice is considered low glycaemia index food it takes longer to cook compared to basmati white rice.

2. White Basmati rice is a starch rich in carbohydrates and B Vitamins.

3. Black Rice is considered a super food because of its high nutritional contents.

4. Red Rice is healthy because it is a white grain making it a good source of fibre and iron.

5. Arborio Rice is good source of iron.

6. Beaten Rice or Poha is rich in dietary fibre and protein, low in calories and rice in iron.

7. Rice noodles- Are gluten free. It is excellent for salads sweets etc.

8. Quinoa – Source of complete protein with a essential amino acids. Even the taste is very good.

9. Cous Cous- This is considered a healthy alternative to pasta since it is made from whole wheat. The calorie value is high.

The Vegetarian

Journey

The Excellent taste of Vegetarian food

Anita Gupta

**The Vegetarian Journey - The Excellent taste of Vegetarian Food
was the first book published by the author.**

CPSIA information can be obtained
at www.ICGtesting.com
Printed in the USA
LVHW072125120220
646444LV00007BA/24

9 781647 835798